Badges
of the
British Army
1820 to the Present

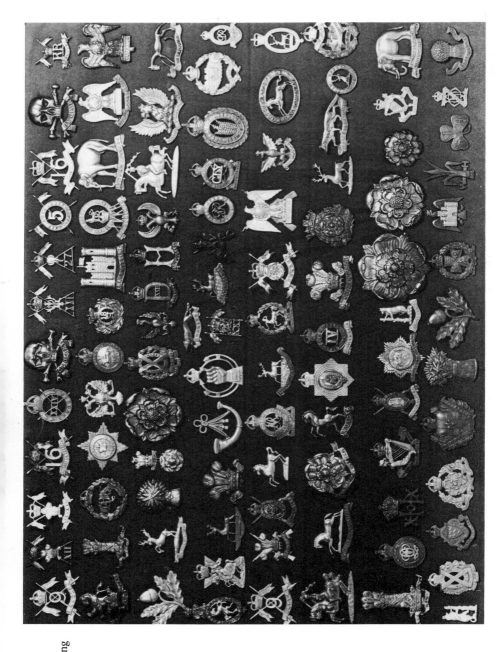

▲ A group of 100 cap and collar badges, mainly cavalry and yeomanry and including some re-strikes which sold for £550 at Sothebys, Sussex in April 1987. (Courtesy Sotheby's, Sussex)

Badges
of the
British Army
1820 to the Present
An Illustrated Reference Guide for Collectors

F. WILKINSON

ARMS AND
ARMOUR

To Teresa and Joanna

Arms and Armour Press
A Cassell Imprint
Wellington House, 125 Strand, London WC2R 0BB.

First published 1969; second edition 1971; third edition 1978;
fourth edition 1980; fifth edition 1982; sixth edition 1984; seventh edition 1987;
reprinted 1992, 1993; eighth edition 1995; ninth edition 1997.

This edition published 1997.
© F. Wilkinson, 1997

British Library Cataloguing-in-Publication Data:
a catalogue record for this book is available from the British Library

ISBN 1-85409-426-2

Designed and edited by DAG Publications Ltd.
Designed by David Gibbons; layout by Anthony A. Evans;
edited by Michael Boxall; photography by Paul Forrester; camerawork
by M&E Reproductions, North Fambridge, Essex;
printed and bound in Great Britain.

Acknowledgements
There are many people to whom the author is, and always will be,
indebted: Jim Burgess, who allowed his collection to be disrupted and
photographed; Paul Forrester, who photographed it and helped in other ways;
Laurie Archer, who was in many ways the founder of the book, and on
whom the author has depended so much; Edmund Greenwood and Roy Butler
of Wallis & Wallis, who supplied much of the extra material in this present
edition. Thanks are also due to many friends and collectors who have been
so kind and generous with their knowledge and advice.

Front of jacket illustration
A selection of British infantry head-dress. The front row
shows various patterns of shako; those in the rear row are Home Service
Pattern helmets. Reproduced by courtesy of Sotheby's.

Contents

Preface

When this book was first discussed in 1968, badge collecting was looked upon as a rather juvenile hobby. There were plenty of badges about, and their prices were low, so there was little challenge in acquiring a good selection of British army badges. School children swapped and traded badges or fixed them on belts as trophies. There was a core of serious collectors, but even they were viewed with a degree of condescension.

Identification of the badges was sometimes a problem and there were few reliable reference sources. Even regimental museums were, on occasions, ignorant of their past 'badge' history. Collectors reported being told that the regiment had never used a certain badge when they had examples and photographic proof of its use. Interest gradually increased, and with this increase came a more dedicated approach. Serious research into pictorial and written evidence was undertaken by collectors. Societies such as the Society for Army Historical Research and the Military Historical Society increased in size, and there was a growing demand for reliable sources and for the collector a bigger market for the badges themselves.

It was not long before commercial interests began to impinge on the market. Old moulds and dies were discovered, new technology offered the ability to create superb copies, and the dreaded re-strike made its appearance. Badges which had been previously thought to be rare were often reproduced in quantity. The problem might not have been too bad if these re-strikes could have been identified for what they were. Unfortunately many were passed off as the original, genuine article. The same

◄ A late 17th-century British military cap with embroidered badge, purchased in a London street market and sold for £6,500 in October 1984. (Courtesy Sotheby's, London)

thing had happened with Third Reich material years before, and both markets are still suffering.

The question of whether a re-strike was acceptable in a collection was debated at length, and there were as many views as there were collectors. It is probably fair to say that the general view was that re-strikes were not quite acceptable and were inferior to the original badge. Dealers and auctioneers generally indicate whether they believe a given example is a re-strike or not. However, it has become increasingly difficult to identify some re-strikes as the technology, skill and knowledge of the suppliers, often from abroad, have improved.

Despite these problems the hobby has grown in importance, and today there are many serious collectors with a deep scholarly interest in the subject. A look at some auction lists will soon confirm the trend, with badges realising prices unheard of a few years ago.

The top prices are obviously achieved by rare items, but even some of the more ordinary pieces will cost in pounds what they cost in pence a few years ago. There is a growing demand for Indian Army items, and prices for this material have rocketed. The changing make-up of the British Army is seeing the disappearance of many long-established regiments and the creation of new ones. The resulting modification of old badges and the adoption of new ones is generating new demands and arrangements.

While headdress badges can be judged to be the most popular area for collectors, there is an expanding demand for associated material badges such as waistbelt clasps, equipment badges, shoulder titles, and even the previously rather despised cloth insignia and buttons now have their collectors.

There is now available a good number of reliable reference books, and it is good to report that the badge collectors bible – Kipling and King – has been reprinted and is again readily available. These volumes will answer the vast majority of queries and are used by many auctioneers and dealers as common reference sources.

The cut-back in defence spending has also led to the closing of some regimental museums. Many have had to dispose of their collections, which has led to an increase in material on the market so that there is always the hope of acquiring that treasure.

For those who want a collecting hobby that is still within the orbit of the collector with limited funds, then badge collecting still has much to offer.

F. Wilkinson, October 1994

Introduction

The present financial climate with its inflation, recession and high taxes has had a marked effect on the antique trade. The prices of most objects have inevitably risen and consequently, for the young enthusiast with very limited means the opportunities to develop a collection of any sort have constantly diminished. In the past bayonets were often the first choice of the schoolboy collector largely because they were cheap. Today even the most common types of such weapons cost more than many young collectors can afford. These decreasing opportunities mean that fewer people are likely to begin collecting. This is an unhappy turn of events for the trade, the collecting community and for the country. The falling number of collectors will mean that, with fewer people taking an active interest, more of the nation's heritage could be lost.

There is however one area in which there are still items available at prices well within the pocket of most people and that is the field of badges. For those at the low-cash end of the collecting market there are badges which can be acquired for very small sums. Even the cheapest can generate hours of research and enjoyment and the rare ones are not impossibly expensive.

When the first edition of this book was written in 1969 badges were, in general, not keenly sought after but there can be no denying that today there is much greater interest. The proliferation of fairs, societies and books dealing with badges and all things military is proof of that.

The study of badges is vast and one of the few that still provides opportunities for research at a basic level. Personal reminiscences, old photographs, regimental museums and memorials can all supply fresh information that is not widely known and which, when published, will be gladly accepted by military historians, collectors, dealers and museums.

The field is wide open, and offers a great choice of possible collecting themes and there are dealers and auction houses ready to supply the needs of collectors. Sadly it must also be admitted that there are some who are only too ready; it cannot be denied that there are a large number of items of dubious quality and authenticity on the market. This means that more than ever collectors need all the information that they can get and it is hoped that this volume will provide some small benefit in this field.

The History of Badges

Badges of one kind or another are vital to the soldier and always have been since failure to distinguish quickly between friend and enemy could mean capture, injury or death. In early times recognition must have been on a personal knowledge basis, but as armies grew in size there had to be some more formal means of recognition. Uniform was an obvious means of identification and units such as the Roman legions would have had a reasonably easy task in distinguishing their friends. What happened in the case of civil war when legion was pitted against legion is not too clear!

The same problem must have existed in the early Middle Ages but from about the 11th century there was developing a simple form of heraldic identification. The system seems to have originated with the use of easily recognizable symbols such as animals, birds, plants and shapes which were adopted by individuals as their personal mark. These symbols were depicted on shields because these were the largest convenient plain surface available for decoration. The same symbols were also used on lead discs which were used to impress the wax seals attached to documents by the nobility to indicate their authenticity. From this simple beginning in the 12th century there developed an enormously elaborate system of heraldry with its own language, customs and rituals.

Under the feudal system, land owners, cities and towns were under an obligation to support their lord and sovereign and supply him with troops when he requested them. It appears from contemporary sources that there gradually developed a system whereby men from a given area were issued with similar costume, in other words a simple style of uniform was beginning to develop.

By the later Middle Ages it was becoming common for lords to dress the men of their household in livery which sported their heraldic coat of arms. Flags, banners and standards were also used to display the arms and here was another thread that was to join with others in the eventual creation of the army uniform. Until the Restoration of Charles II in 1660 there was no regular body that could be called a formal or standing army and in consequence there could be no central control over the dress of the troops. Each unit or regiment was, up to a point, a law unto itself.

During the English Civil Wars (1642–9) the two opposing armies,

Parliament and Royalists, were hard to distinguish one from another since their arms, equipment and dress were very similar. Obviously this was not helpful when battle was joined. One solution was a general instruction, prior to the battle, to adopt some form of recognition symbol which might be as simple as a twig pushed into a hatband. Another and more formal system was to wrap a coloured scarf around the waist or drape it across the shoulder. There can be little doubt that there were moments when systems such as these failed and there must have been encounters that turned out to be friend against friend.

Following the Restoration Parliament, with many misgivings, agreed to set up a standing army and herein lies the beginning of the regular British army. Each unit or regiment was under the control of a Colonel and his was the ruling hand. The regiment took his name or a title chosen by him as with Colonel, the Earl of Plymouth's Regiment of Horse (later the 3rd Dragoon Guards) or Colonel, the Duke of Beaufort's Musketeers (later the Devonshire Regiment). Since the commanding officer was titled he was naturally the proud owner of a coat of arms which was generally adopted as the distinguishing symbol of the regiment. During the 16th century there are references to 'The Queen's Badge' but it is not clear if these were the royal arms or another device. If the colonel were killed or left the regiment, the name of the regiment would change and a new coat of arms could be the adopted emblem. In general this system of naming continued until 1751.

In 1747 the Duke of Cumberland ordered that the colour or flag of each regiment should include in its design a number, either painted or embroidered, indicating its position in the order of precedence of the various regiments. The figure was to be in the form of a Roman numeral and the correct number had to be confirmed by the Secretary-at-War. Gradually the regiments began referring to themselves by this number and thus the Devonshire Regiment would tend to be referred to as the 11th. In 1751 the position was regularized by a Royal Warrant and for the next century or so the regiments were known by their number, later modified in some cases by the addition of a county connection.

The regimental arms had been placed on pieces of equipment and were embroidered on to coats, holsters and horse trappings, but in the 17th century they were not commonly placed on the three-cornered or wide-brimmed hats. The first exception seems to have been with the caps of the Grenadiers. These troops were, at first, specialists in the use of small hand-thrown bombs or grenades and in order that their throwing action should not be impeded they avoided the wide-brimmed hat and wore a tall fur cap with a stiffened front flap. This plain area was soon inviting some form of decoration and contemporary illustrations indicate a range of motifs including the royal arms, grenades and national emblems such as the shamrock.

The use of the Colonel's arms was expressly forbidden in the

▲ Left: A Tarleton Helmet of the Light Horse Volunteers. Right: A Regency bell-topped Shako of the 8th Royal Veterans Battalion. Both good examples of early British headdress. (Courtesy Wallis & Wallis)

▼ The large brass General Pattern badge from a Waterloo Shako, die-stamped with the intertwining 'GR'. Other regimental issues would have included approved devices.

▼ A very fine example of the 1830 Pattern Bell Top Officer's Shako of the 34th (Cumberland) Regiment of Foot. The large badge has a green enamel centre and includes the battle honour 'Ava'. Sold for £572 in January 1987. (Courtesy Sotheby's, Sussex)

▲ An exceptionally fine 1843 helmet of the 5th (Inniskilling) Dragoons. It is of brass with its horsehair plume and large plate fitted to this type of helmet. A rare piece which in November 1988 sold for £1,450. (Courtesy of Wallis & Wallis)

▶▲ A Shako of about 1831–50 as worn by the South Herts Yeomanry. It has lines which were attached to the tunic to prevent accidental loss. (Courtesy Sotheby's, London)

◀ An officer's Albert Shako c. 1850. The badge lacks the centre piece so preventing a regimental identification. This reduces its value slightly, but it sold for £990 in February 1989. (Courtesy Sotheby's, Sussex)

▼ All from a sale of May 1989; left to right: Shako of an officer of The Renfrew Militia (The Prince of Wales's Royal Regiment). This example has the name of the owner written inside and the date Jan. 1863. Sold for £440. An officer's Blue Cloth Home Service Helmet of the 3rd Lanarkshire Rifle Volunteers. The helmet plate has the Imperial crown which means that it post-dates 1902. Sold for £510. An officer's Shako of the 1869 Pattern for the Hampshire Militia and consequently the lace and badge are silver in colour. Sold for £410. (Courtesy Wallis & Wallis)

Warrant of 1751 which uses for the first time the term 'badge' and goes into details of the various regimental emblems. The devices were painted on various items or embroidered with coloured worsted on to caps and clothing.

In the middle of the 18th century, although the royal cipher was still in general use, there was developing the use of symbols. The 18th-century English artist William Hogarth in his painting 'March of the Guards to Finchley' shows a pioneer wearing a hat whose brim is embroidered with a pickaxe and a saw, tools of his military trade.

At the same time there was an increasing use of metal badges especially on leather cartridge pouches but also on some headdress. Firm evidence for this practice is provided by a Clothing Warrant of 1768 which goes into details of the Grenadiers' badge to be worn on their fur caps. It was to be fixed to the front of the black bearskin cap and was to be of silver-plated metal on a black ground with the king's crest and the motto *Nec Espera Terrent*. The Grenadiers' caps were also to have a grenade badge at the back with the number of the regiment on it. How general the use of metal badges was is difficult to assess because the same Warrant talks of other hats and does not mention badges at all.

Changes in the style of military headdress were taking place during this period, and in the 1760s the Fusiliers were issued with a leather, helmet-shaped hat the front of which was fitted with a white-metal plate or badge. The Light Dragoons were also adopting helmets of various types, and paintings and literary references indicate that some of these had metal badges fitted at the front. By the 1780s the Light Dragoons were wearing quite elaborate helmets with turbans, peaks and fur crests and many of these had quite large metal badges fitted on the side of the helmet.

Infantry, with the exception of the grenadiers, mostly retained their tricorn hats throughout the 18th century, but a big change was at hand. In Hungary the Magyars had long worn a tall, cylinder-like hat to which had been fitted a peak which helped shelter the face from wind and rain. It had been copied by Austrian troops and in 1800 an order dated 24 February announced that the shako, a variously spelt version of the original Hungarian word, would become standard for most of the British infantry.

It was eight inches tall and its shape has gained it the nickname of the Stovepipe Shako. It was decorated with a rosette on the front at the centre of which was a regimental button and behind was a feather plume. The colour of the plume was red and white for most troops, dark-green for the Light Companies and white for the Grenadiers. The front was also adorned with a plate approximately 6 inches by 4 inches stamped with a crowned GR within the Garter, surmounting a lion and surrounded with military trophies. Regiments were allowed to modify the design and include their number or special symbols. The brass plate was secured to the body of the shako by wire loops through the corners and the officers' version of copper-gilt had small looped lugs on the back.

The new shako was found to be less than satisfactory and in March 1812 its design was changed to the so-called Waterloo Shako. The first difference was to make the body of felt instead of the previous, rather heavy, lacquered material. Its height was reduced to just over 6 inches although it was fitted with a false front slightly above 8 inches high.

Dragoons c. 1855 – £200. Post-1802 helmet plate of Royal Irish Regiment – £130. (Courtesy Wallis & Wallis)

▲ A Blue Cloth helmet of the 2nd Battalion The West Yorkshire Regiment. The plate has the Queen's crown with the high side arms and this feature dates it before Queen Victoria's death and the change of crown in 1902. Sold for £400

in August 1989. (Courtesy Wallis & Wallis)

▼ All from a sale of August 1989; left to right: Post-1902 helmet plate of The 7th City of London Regiment – £155. Victorian Shako plate of the 4th (Queen's Own) Light

▲ Blue cloth helmet of the Royal Army Medical Corps showing the ball and cup fitting worn by the various corps. Sold for £270; a higher price than that for a regimental one in similar condition. (Courtesy Wallis & Wallis)

The central plume was moved to the left and the button was altered for Light and Grenadier companies to a bugle-horn and a grenade. A new feature was a plaited worsted cord, white for other ranks and gold and crimson for officers, which was draped across the front of the shako. Light Infantry were distinguished by a green cord.

The smaller shako called for a smaller badge, the shape of which was shield-like with a crown at the top. The general design was simpler with an intertwined GR above a regimental number; regiments with allocated devices were allowed to use them but most incorporated the crowned GR.

The Waterloo Shako was in service for only four years; in August 1816 a new style of headdress was adopted. The new headdress was far more extravagant than the previous patterns, possibly as a result of the close contact with the rather glamorous uniforms of the Allies and the French during the occupation of France following the defeat of Napoleon. The Regency Shako of black felt widened towards the crown and was fitted with a polished leather peak and a tall, 12-inch plume behind a central cockade. The shako could be held in place on the head by tying, under the chin, the tapes of two sets of overlapping metal scales which formed a kind of chin-strap.

Despite the elaborate hat, the badge was relatively simple and was basically no more than a gilt or silver disc with a crown above it. For the officers the disc carried the regimental badge or number; the other ranks' badge was simpler and carried only the number.

In 1822 the officers' shako was modified, being made slightly taller and the badge was now far more elaborate. It now consisted of a large, usually silver, star which varied somewhat in style with a central circular section which was made up of the regimental badge. The other big departure from previous styles was the inclusion of battle honours in the badge design.

In 1829 the shako underwent yet another change when the so-called bell-topped model was introduced. This was considerably wider at the top than the previous type and that for officers had a leather top. As it was a new style a new type of badge was inevitable and this was much larger. Basically it consisted of the old-style silver badge with an even larger gilt, star-shaped plate surmounted by a crown behind it. For other ranks a simpler, die-stamped star and crown plate with the regimental number at the centre was introduced, but this was replaced in 1839 by a circular plate with a crown and regimental number. The plume was retained, but in 1831 was reduced in height and in 1833 it was replaced by a worsted ball.

In 1844 the Albert Shako, so-called after the Prince Regent, was adopted and this in some ways was a reversion to the earlier form. It was cylindrical with a peak at the front and a smaller one at the back, and at the sides two large rosettes secured the ends of a chin-chain. The other ranks' shako was similar in shape but had only a black leather chin-strap and the badge was rather like that on the Regency

Shako, consisting of a brass disc with a surmounting crown and a border made up of laurel and oak leaves with the regimental number in the centre.

The officers' badge was far more elaborate with an eight-pointed gilt star, the top centre point being replaced by a crown. The main arms of the star often carried battle honours of the regiment. Superimposed on the star was a wreath, half of laurel leaves and half of palm leaves, and within this was the regimental badge. As usual there were distinctions for the Grenadier and Light companies.

The Albert Shako was soon found to be less than satisfactory and it was finally disgraced during the Crimean War (1854–6) when it proved to be clumsy, offered poor protection and was generally useless; the simpler, more practical forage cap was found to be far more sensible. Even the rather hide-bound British high command could not ignore the fact that the headdress was largely useless. No doubt influenced by the French who were, for once, their allies, they decided that tall hats were out and a smaller, less unbalanced pattern was required and they chose a French style look-alike kepi. In January 1855 the new, low-crowned shako was approved. It was only just over 5 inches tall at the front and curved down over the back of the head. It had a bigger and squarer front peak than the Albert, but retained that model's back peak, black chin-strap and worsted ball.

The lower crown meant that a smaller style of badge was needed, but the basic design of the Albert pattern remained. The eight-pointed star with a crown was kept and the centre carried the regimental number within the Garter with the motto *Honi soit qui mal y pense*. The officers' plate was pierced, that of the other ranks was stamped, but there were many minor variations on this basic pattern.

Six years after its adoption this shako was discarded and a new form of similar shape was introduced. The main body was of cork and to this was attached a covering of blue cloth which was held in place by lines of stitching. This feature has given it the title of the quilted shako. In general shape it was not greatly different from its predecessor although it was slightly shorter and the back peak was abolished. The badge was slightly smaller than the previous one, but had the same features with a star, crown and regimental numbers. Apart from its size, the main differences were that the quilted shako had bands of regimental lace around the top to indicate the wearer's rank, and the motto was no longer pierced. As with every 'standard' badge introduced by the authorities there were regimental variations.

The next change came in June 1869 when yet another variant was adopted, but this featured only differences in detail, the basic shape remaining much the same. There was, however, a big change in the badge and the star which had been in use since the bell-topped shako was dropped. In its place came a version similar to the central section of the old Albert Shako plate. A wreath of laurel, surmounted by a crown, enclosed the Garter with its motto and inside that was the

▲ All from July 1989 sale; left to right: An officer's Maltese Cross shako plate of The 3rd (King's Own) Light Dragoons – £270. Officer's shako plate of The 20th (Worcestershire) Regiment

c. 1869 – £60. Victorian officer's helmet plate of The 6th Lancashire (1st Manchester) Rifle Volunteer Corps – £125.
►▼ A Victorian officer's lance cap of the 12th (Prince of

Wales's Royal) Lancers, which should have a drooping cluster of scarlet swan's feathers. Such a piece would probably sell for about £2,000. (Courtesy Sotheby's, London)

▲ An NCO of the 6th Lancashire (1st Manchester) Rifle Volunteer Corps, wearing the peaked forage cap with the regimental numeral in brass.

► Rank and file helmet plate from the lance cap of the 9th Queen's Royal Lancers. The King's crown dates it to post-1902.

regimental number. Its size was very similar to the previous plate. The most obvious difference in the shako itself was the adoption of a chin-chain with a velvet backing which, when not worn, could be looped up on a hook positioned at the centre of the back crown.

The period from 1860 to 1880 was remarkable for the changes in military equipment and tactics. The Prussians scored the breath-taking victories in a series of campaigns against the Danes, the Austrians and then the mighty French. Their new breech-loading rifles made a tremendous impact on all military thought. The Prussians were regarded with fear and awe. Their success made them the 'stars' of warfare and it may well have been this influence that caused the British authorities to bring in the next and biggest change to British Army headdress.

Since the 1840s the Prussians had favoured a helmet with a central top spike. In the 1860s even the Metropolitan Police had doffed their top hats and adopted the present helmet based on the Prussian form which was to be copied later by most other forces. In June 1877 an order was issued stating that overseas officers would wear a white cork helmet without puggaree (the turban-like wrapping around the base). The badge was to be a large helmet plate reverting to the older star and crown with a laurel wreath, the Garter and motto and in the centre the regimental number or special regimental device. Many included regimental battle honours. In May 1878 the new helmet became the general full dress wear.

It was of cork with a covering of blue cloth for most units and green for Light Infantry units, with peaks back and front and a chin-chain. The top was surmounted by a spike or, in the case of the various corps such as the Artillery and Engineers, a ball in a leaf cup. A chin-chain of rings was draped across the front which could be hooked up at the back when not in use.

For the new helmet the earlier star and crown style badge came back into use with the regimental number at the centre of a laurel wreath, the Garter and the motto. It was large, being some 5 inches tall and more than 4 inches wide. As before, the various regimental devices could be incorporated with the number. The Rifle and Fusilier regiments had their own special patterns; for example, the 60th Foot having a Maltese Cross in place of the star.

In December 1868 Edward Cardwell, a former Colonial Secretary, was appointed Secretary of State for War. He set about reforming an army that was in difficulties. Despite much opposition he introduced such reforms as the abolition of the purchase of commissions. Flogging was abolished and, influenced by the Prussian system, he proposed that the country be divided into 66 territorial districts. Regiments would be allocated a district from which, it was hoped, they would draw their recruits. There was also to be a closer association with local units of militia and volunteers. Although Cardwell left office in February 1874, his influence was to have a profound effect on the

▲ Sealed pattern caps which were sent out to the manufacturers as standard samples to copy. That on the left is for the 1896 Glengarry and the other is for the Infantry Officer of the Line Regiment forage cap, again dated 1895.

▶▲Contemporary photograph from time of the South African War showing the slouch hat favoured at that period. The unit is probably the City of London (Rough Riders) one of the Imperial Yeomanry units.

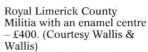

▲ Shoulder belt plates from a sale of November 1988. Top, officer's shoulder belt plate of a Volunteer Battalion of the Gordon Highlanders. It is distinguished from that for Regular officers by the fact that the names are missing below the Sphinx and Tiger – battle honours of the regulars – £80. Left, a similar plate for a Volunteer officer of The Queen's Own Cameron Highlanders, again with a blank battle honour – £150. Right: an officer's plate of the Royal Limerick County Militia with an enamel centre – £400. (Courtesy Wallis & Wallis)

▲ Horse furniture fittings. Top: Stirrup leather slider in white-metal; remainder brass bosses from the harness.

design of regimental badges.

In 1881 the then Secretary of State for War, Hugh Childers, promulgated Cardwell's ideas in an even more drastic form; in future regiments would be known by their territorial title. Although not specifically stated in the General Order of May 1881, the old numbers of precedence would no longer be used and some regiments would be amalgamated. The shock to the regiments was enormous but the reform went through.

This order meant new badges, the numbers being replaced by the new titles. The basic shape of the badge was unaltered but the centre, which had previously held the regimental number, was now filled by the regimental emblem and often the motto as well.

The helmet plate was to remain unchanged until 1902 when, following the death of Queen Victoria, the crown was altered. The Victorian crown with its high curving arms was replaced by the Imperial crown with its down-swept arms. There were some changes to the centre plate for some regiments.

The helmet plates for other ranks were of brass and most were of two pieces – the star and crown plate and a circular centre piece which was attached by wire loops on the back.

The badges mentioned above were all worn for full dress occasions and in the case of the earlier patterns they were worn at all times. Later it became common to have a less 'formal' headdress worn when full dress was inappropriate. The cavalry had long had a cap originally worn when collecting fodder for the horses and the Warrant of 1768 mentions a watering cap. The 1795 Standing orders of the 2nd Queen's Dragoon Guards makes a clear distinction between hats and caps, specifying when each should be worn. A 'System for the Compleat Interior Management and Economy of a Battalion of Infantry' of 1768 states that the troops are to wear foraging caps for many occasions. A volume of 1777 enjoins the troops to make their foraging cap out of their old coat. The fodder or forage cap became general undress wear and the cavalry pattern was a plain round 'pillbox' style whereas the infantry officers had a peak. In 1898 the present style of peaked cap in the well-known form with a wide circular top was introduced. In 1902 another cap of similar shape but lacking the peak was introduced for other ranks. Named the Brodrick after Sir John Brodrick it was not popular and was made obsolete for infantry in 1905 although the Royal Marine Light Infantry retained theirs.

In 1868 a Scottish-style bonnet, the glengarry, was adopted by all infantry for undress wear. It was worn by English regiments until the 1890s and had a much smaller badge than the helmet plate. It was in fact the centre of the helmet plate worn as a separate item. Many but by no means all were made up of the ribbon of the Garter enclosing the number or the badge of the regiment. After the change to Territorial titles in 1881 the badges were changed and the number disappeared. Another type of Scottish headdress was the Kilmarnock which was a beret-type hat with a band around the head. This was worn by British troops from about 1812 to 1874.

The forage cap was not the only alternative headdress; the Field cap was a flat, folding cloth cap originally intended for wear on manoeuvres and active service. In 1888 a flat folding cap was issued for all troops who normally wore the forage cap, and in 1894 it was taken into general use. In 1937 a coloured version of the Field cap was introduced in which the colour of the crown was an indication of regiment.

In 1902 the South African War led to the adoption of the slouch hat with the wide brim turned up at one side but its use lapsed. It was probably inspired by the Colonial troops who served in that war.

Following the First World War there was a trend toward more practical uniform and accessories and in 1924 a black beret was approved for members of the Tank Corps and then in 1943 the Parachute Regiment was granted a red beret and the Commandos a green one. A khaki version was also issued to Irish troops in the same year.

While the infantry regiments had been mauled by the reforms of 1881, the cavalry was largely unaffected. They retained their numbers and these were displayed on the helmet plates. A variety of metal helmets was worn by the cavalry, but the large plates remained basically the same with an eight-, later twelve-pointed star with the Garter at the centre with the number or emblem.

British cavalry had consisted largely of heavy units and Light Dragoons until 1816 when, inspired by Napoleon's use of them, the cavalry introduced lancers. Their uniform and headdress was adapted from the Polish style which included the lance cap or *czapka* (also *shapska, tchapka,* etc.) The top widened into a square flat top and the lower leather section was fitted with a large curved triangular plate with a scalloped edge. It was embossed with radiating rays and battle honours and the regimental emblem and title. The officers' version was much more elaborate but of the same form.

Smaller versions of many of the cap badges were adopted for wear on the collar in 1874 and these will be found in pairs and, in the case of animals, will face inwards to the opening of the collar.

While the vast majority of cap and headdress badges were of metal, many cloth or embroidered badges were worn in the British army. The earliest badges were often embroidered and during the 19th century a series of sleeve badges was introduced. They were used to indicate the trade or skill of a soldier and comprised patches with appropriate symbols such as crossed rifles for a marksman or weapons instructor, crossed flags for a signaller or a drum for a drummer. There were also embroidered regimental titles stitched at the top of the sleeve of the jacket or blouse. Other versions were made to slip over epaulettes. In 1907 a metal version of these regimental titles was introduced and these were worn at the base of the epaulette.

During the First World War another cloth identification was adopted and this indicated the division to which the soldier or vehicle belonged and this was stitched at the top of the sleeve. The divisional patch was abandoned after the war but was re-introduced in 1940 during the Second World War.

There were many other styles of regimental badges used in the British army including some attractive horse furniture fittings details of which were all set down in the official Dress Regulations which were periodically revised and re-issued.

Changes in the style of warfare and armies meant that often items of equipment were discarded as being no longer relevant. In the case of the cavalry the sabretache was abandoned in 1902 after about a century of wear. Originally intended as a kind of detached pocket, because many tight-fitting cavalry uniforms did not really accommodate them, the sabretache was attached to the sword belt and usually carried an elaborately decorated regimental badge.

Another casualty was the attractive shoulder belt plate or, in contemporary terms, the breast plate. This was a fitting which linked the belt carrying the sword or bayonet which had originally circled the waist. During the period beginning with the War of American Independence there was a gradual change to a belt which crossed over the shoulder. This positioned the plate at the centre of the chest and a new style of fitting was developed. The early examples mostly were oval and had an engraved design. The shape was gradually changed and during the 19th century was largely rectangular. Those for the rank and file were usually simply stamped out of brass, but the officers' pattern became very elaborate with the design being made up of several pieces including battle honours. They were finally abandoned in 1855. The Scottish regiments retained theirs which are usually of white-metal.

◄ During the Napoleonic Wars a large number of Volunteer units were formed and they all designed their various badges. These shoulder belt plates are all of volunteer units. The oval shape suggests that they date from early in the 19th century. The lower one, together with a belt fitting, is for the Westminster Light Horse.

Collecting Badges

The brief history of British Army badges gives some idea of the scope of badge collecting. It is without doubt one of the few 'cheap' collecting fields still available with prices ranging from a few pence to hundreds of pounds. It is obvious that the older a badge is the more likely it is to be expensive. However other considerations such as condition will affect price as will rarity generated by a short period of use. Units were created, disbanded and amalgamated, sometimes all within a short period so that their badge was in service but briefly. Such units' badges are correspondingly scarce and in greater demand.

Condition is important; it is not unknown for badges to have been converted to brooches or menu-holders, or fitted to napkin-rings. A rare badge may have been rescued from such use and re-converted and as such can be considered less desirable than an unchanged example.

One factor that affects the price of a badge is the regiment concerned; one with a long, distinguished history will usually, subject to the comments above, be more expensive than a badge of a non-combatant unit. Similarly officers' badges will usually be of better quality and so more expensive. The prices quoted in the list are the mid-range, ordinary example value and as such should be treated with caution since they are in no way absolute. They are indicators and no more, and examples will be encountered with prices quoted well above or below the figure included in the list.

Where to find the badges? There are several auction houses that handle smaller items such as badges and these are to be supported. For the purchaser there is an insurance that should the object be found defective in some way, the auctioneers will refund or otherwise compensate. The best-known auction rooms which handle badges on a fairly regular basis are Wallis & Wallis of Lewes, Kent Sales, Phillips and Bonhams. There are other rooms that may well have occasional lots of badges.

There are dealers who specialize and send out lists and these can be extremely reliable, but how does the beginner know which to trust? The first step is to make contact with fellow collectors because word-of-mouth is still one of the best means of finding the good dealers.

There are a number of societies catering for military collectors and details of local branches or exhibitions, fairs and sales can often be found at the local library or museum. Details of the societies are also given in some of the military-interest magazines generally available from booksellers and newsagents.

Having decided to collect badges, how to decide whether the example is worth the asking price? Alas there is no easy answer! Every item is worth what somebody is prepared to pay and if a specimen is wanted enough the asking price will be paid. What to look for when deciding on the price? Condition is fairly obvious, but is the piece a genuine article? It is a good policy to expect every piece to be wrong and then convince oneself that it is right rather than the other way round. Look at the fitting and see if it is likely to be a replacement. Examine the piece for breaks and repairs. A good magnifying-glass is well worth using when examining a specimen for there may be small defects not visible to the unaided eye.

Fortunately, for beginners there are now available a number of reliable books with clear illustrations of the various badges and good descriptions. However the book which illustrates every possible badge will never be written. There have been, are and always will be variations on a theme. The regulations may define a badge, but the manufacturer may have deviated slightly, or the regiment or battalion may have claimed an exemption to the rules. In some cases the badge may not even be recorded and it has been known for a regimental museum to deny the existence of a proved genuine badge of that unit. Thus the badge being offered may well be totally genuine but just slightly different; the spelling of the name may vary slightly; the position of one feature may be slightly different. In the end it must be a matter of opinion until research from old photographs and other sources proves the case one way or other.

The material may also vary since the usual badge may be of brass but it is not impossible to find a variant of bimetal form, that is, with parts of brass and white-metal. Brass was the commonest material but external pressures have sometimes forced changes. In 1942, during the Second World War, in order to conserve stocks of metal, badges were manufactured from plastic. These plastic badges were basically copies of the original metal regimental badge and were produced in silver, bronze and dark-brown colours with one or two in black. In 1952 another type of material, Staybrite, with a rather cheap and shiny look to it, was substituted.

The regular army units normally had their badge in brass or gilt metal for officers, while the militia, a form of reserve force, had theirs in white-metal or silver. Many regular Scottish regiments differed in that their badges were in white-metal. In the case of other ranks the badges were normally die-stamped from a single piece of metal but those for officers were more elaborate with the central, regimental, insignia made separately and held in place by wire or small rods passing through lugs on the back of the badge. Because the Glengarry, when introduced, was for 'off-duty' wear or undress, officers' badges were usually embroidered on the side.

Many badges incorporated a crown, a feature which was retained when other details were altered. The shape of the crown was changed

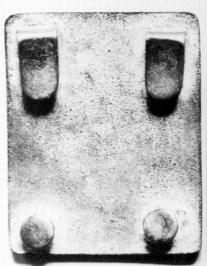
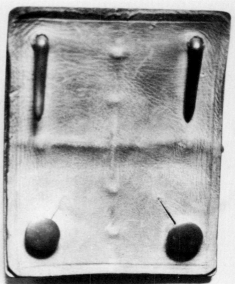

▲ The backs of shoulder belt plates showing the typical fittings to engage with the belt.

▼ A selection of badges from just one unit, the 9th (East Norfolk) Regiment of Foot.

whenever a new sovereign came to the throne and the crown and cipher are useful in giving a rough date to a badge.

Most metal badges were secured to the headdress by lugs, two on the smaller ones and three or four on the larger ones. These lugs were looped at the tip and passed through the material of the cap or shako and either a brass split-pin or a thin wedge of leather was pushed through the loop to hold the badge in position.

When the Brodrick was introduced and later the peaked Field Service cap, their badges had a different kind of fitting known as a slider. This was a narrow, flat bar running parallel with the badge but standing slightly away from the back which slipped into a slit in the material of the cap.

The regimental insignia featured on British cap badges has evolved from a variety of sources. Some are reminders of previous campaigns such as the Sphinx on the badge of the Gloucestershire Regiment with the title 'Egypt'. Another is the French eagle captured during the Napoleonic Wars and used on the badge of The Royal Scots Greys (2nd Dragoons). Other badges incorporate some landmark associated with the area from which the regiment takes its name such as the castle on the Royal Inniskilling Fusiliers. All these features and associations offer scope for research and follow-up work.

Apart from the badges of the armed forces there are many other types, both official and unofficial, including those known as Sweetheart badges. These are essentially decorative civilian versions of the official badge. The copies are usually smaller than the actual service badge, some are enamelled, some had gold, silver and even diamond fittings and most have pin fittings. The sweetheart badges were those worn by wives and sweethearts as mementoes of brothers, husbands and boyfriends serving in the forces.

Badges were, at one time, the happy hunting-ground of boys and impecunious collectors, but as interest spread, demand increased and prices naturally rose and have continued to do so. The demand has been such that some dealers and others feel it incumbent on themselves to help satisfy it. This they have done by producing 're-strikes' which have become the bane of the badge collector. These are simply modern copies of a badge sometimes struck from the original die or from a specially made die, or produced from modern casting techniques. So good are most of these re-strikes that it is difficult to distinguish the genuine from the copy. The number of varieties is quite extensive ranging from early 19th-century badges to rare 20th-century examples.

It is, unfortunately, impossible to give an infallible rule for distinguishing re-strikes. Quality has improved and in a few years' time with some genuine wear it is going to be impossible to know which is the original. It is possible to distinguish some by the slightly inferior quality of the detail and on some the lugs at the back are rather crudely fitted.

▼ The cavalry were often a little more glamorous and garish in the uniform accessories and these two back pouches are typical.

The pouch flaps and fittings on the belt are of hallmarked silver (Birmingham, 1899–1900) and the right one Birmingham, 1880.

Hampshire Yeomanry Cavalry – £350. Right, West Somerset Yeomanry – £140. Both sold in June 1989. (Courtesy Wallis & Wallis)

▼ There is growing interest in the badges of the Indian Army and prices are rising very quickly. These two items clearly demonstrate the difference. Left, a Victorian

officer's belt and back pouch of the 6th (Burma) Bn 31st Madras Light Infantry; the silver fittings hall-marked for Birmingham 1897–8 sold for £725. The Lancers' back

pouch with a silver flap hall-marked for Birmingham 1875 sold for £210. (Courtesy Wallis & Wallis)

What hope for the collector then? Experience is the key and if a collector lacks his own then he should use that of other people. Take every opportunity to handle genuine badges. Examine them through a magnifying-glass and see if they have the small pits caused by inferior casting or stamping. Examine the detail; some re-strikes lack fine finish. Compare it with any known genuine example although this is often not possible when confronted by the piece in the shop or market. In this situation trust in the dealer is vital.

The ethics of re-strikes is a constant topic of discussion among collectors and if there is a general consensus it is that, if offered and sold as re-strikes, they might be acceptable. What is inexcusable is the sale of re-strikes as originals. Many collectors reluctantly accept examples in their collections since the genuine example is so rare and expensive that they feel they will never find or afford one.

Despite these problems badge collecting is still by present-day standards, a comparatively cheap branch of militaria unless the collector seeks the very rare examples. Cloth insignia are probably the cheapest of all and modern examples are fairly plentiful and they make an attractive display.

In addition to all the various armed forces badges of all countries there are scores of other badges. Disabled groups, veterans, various bodies such as the Army Temperance Association all issued badges of various shapes and sizes. Although less popular than the better-known types, they do have one great advantage for they are usually cheaper!

To the general public badges are still regarded as commonplace, and at jumble-sales, boot-sales and similar events they may still be had at very reasonable prices. Auction houses and specialist dealers are all well aware of their value and bargains are scarce. The advantage of using these sources is only the 'guarantee' of authenticity and exchange of dubious purchases. Unfortunately the re-strikes are so good that even experts may differ as to their genuineness and in the end it is a matter of opinion.

As a collection is built up there comes the time to display it and this can be a problem since the display will often be changing as new or better examples are acquired. In the past many good badges have been ruined by the bending, removal, drilling and nailing of the sliders and lugs and this must be avoided at all costs. Cloth insignia can be stitched to a material backing although this obviously causes wear and possibly damage. Double-sided sticky tape is another possibility as well as small blobs of the various proprietary materials such as Blue Tack. If these are used it is as well to check that there is no potential chemical reaction between cloth and adhesives and that it can be removed without any adverse effect.

If the badges are to be displayed probably the simplest method is to cover a polystyrene tile with an appropriate coloured material or paper. The lugs can then be gently pressed in the tile or if the badge is fitted with a slider this can be slipped into the material. This system should cause no damage to the badges and can be very easily changed if new badges are acquired or the theme is changed.

Cleaning needs to be kept to a minimum since the rubbing will gradually diminish the detail as instanced by some of the genuine examples which have seen service and been cleaned regularly. Patent fluid cleaners are available and as always it is as well to test them on an unimportant badge before chancing it on quality examples.

Although the individual costs of the badges may be small, the value of a collection soon builds up and as such they should be insured. A full description of the badge should be kept and it is common to use the number in one of the standard reference books such as Kipling & King as a good identification. If a photograph is contemplated it should be remembered that a reasonable close-up picture is preferable to a general view of a number.

Bibliography

For the collector of British army material there are several books which will answer most everyday queries and are of prime importance. For the broad history of the British army there is no equal to Fortescue's massive work. Some of the incidental detail has since been found to be somewhat suspect, but it is still a monumental work. There are problems in consulting this work for it runs to many volumes and has long been out of print although there has been at least one reprint. This means that most collectors will have to rely on libraries and probably specialist ones at that.

For general details of the broad history of the British Army there are many other books available. For the details of the various changes of title of regiments Farmer, Chichester and Parkyn are good reliable sources.

For uniforms any title by Carman is bound to be of use and his books are good all-round works. For headdress badges the definitive reference is the two-volume work by Kipling and King.

This is by no means an exhaustive bibliography but seeks to list those volumes which are reasonably easy to acquire or consult and are of most general use. Many of the books listed contain extensive bibliographies which will help point the reader towards more specialist publications.

Several of the main institutions concerned with military history have very extensive libraries and, within certain guide-lines and limitations of staff, will allow serious students and collectors access to them. Usually an appointment will be necessary so that it is essential to write or telephone in advance to check the position. Written inquiries are also dealt with but in these days of limited staff and facilities there is likely to be some delay in receiving a reply. If information is being sought by letter the request should be as specific as possible. If identification of an object is sought, a polaroid or competent sketch is more or less essential; verbal descriptions can be very vague and confusing.

Addresses of the various museums can be found in many publications available at most libraries. Regimental museums are frequently staffed by part-time curators whose time is usually well filled and replies to queries can be rather slow in coming.

An asterisk indicates that the book has been reprinted at some time.

Adair, R. *British Eighth Army in North Africa*. London, 1974

Alastair, Campbell D. *The Dress of the Royal Artillery*. London, 1971

Anderson, D. *Scots in Uniform*. Edinburgh, 1972

Bloomer, W. H., and K. D. *Scottish Regimental Badges, 1793–1971*. London, 1973

Bowling, A. H. *Scottish Regiments, 1660–1914*. London, 1970

Carman, W. Y. *Indian Army Uniforms – Cavalry*. London, 1961

— *Indian Army Uniforms – Infantry*. London, 1969

— *British Military Uniforms from Contemporary Pictures*. London, 1968

— *A Dictionary of Military Uniform*. London, 1977

— *Headdresses of the British Army – Cavalry*. Sandhurst, 1968

— *Headdresses of the British Army – Yeomanry*. London, 1970

— *Glengarry Badges of the British Line Regiments*. London, 1973

Chichester, H. and Burgess Short, G. *Records and Badges of Every Regiment and Corps in the British Army*. London, 1976*

Churchill, C. and Westlake, R. *British Army Collar Badges, 1881 to the Present*. London, 1986

Clammer, D. *The Victorian Army in Photographs*. London, 1975

Cockle, M. J. *Bibliography of English Books up to 1642*. Reprint London, 1976

Cole, H. *Badges on Battledress*. London, 1953

— *Formation Badges of World War II*. London, 1973

Cox, R. *Military Badges of the British Empire, 1914–18*. London, 1982

Crookshank, C de W. *Prints of British Military Operations*. London, 1921

Davies, H. P. *British Parachute Forces, 1940–45*. London, 1974

Davis, L. D. *British Army Cloth Insignia, 1940 to the Present*. London, 1988

Dress Regulations: 1846, repr. London, 1971; *1857*, repr. London, 1976; *1900*, repr. London, 1969

Edwards, T. *Regimental Badges*. 5th edn London, 1968

Ewing, E. *Women in Uniform*. London, 1976

Frederick, J. *Lineage Book of the British Army*. London, 1969

Fortescue, J. *History of the British Army*. London, 1899–1930*

Gaylor, J. *Military Badge Collecting*. London, 1971*

Harris, R. G. *50 Years of Yeomanry Uniforms*. London, 1972

Haswell-Miller, A. and Dawnay, N. *Military Drawings and Paintings in the Royal Collection*. 2 vols. London, 1966 and 1970

Haythornthwaite, P. *Uniforms of the Napoleonic Wars*. London, 1973

— *Uniforms of the Peninsular War, 1807–14*. Poole, 1978

— *World Uniforms and Battles, 1815–50*. Poole, 1976

Higham, R. A. *A Guide to Sources of British Military*

History. London, 1972

Hutchinson & Co. *The Army in India*. London, 1968

Johnson, S. *Chats on Military Curios*. London, 1915

Kannik, P. *Military Uniforms in Colour*. London, 1967

Katcher, P. *King George's Army, 1775–1783*. London, 1973

Kipling, A. and King, H. *Headdress Badges of the British Army*. 2 vols. London, 1973 and 1979

Knotel, H. and R. *Uniforms of the World*. London, 1980

Lawson, H. *A History of the Uniforms of the British Army*. 5 vols. London, 1962–7

Leslie, N. *The Succession of Colonels of the British Army from 1660*. London, 1974

Luard, J. *History of the Dress of the British Soldier*. London, 1852*

Lyndhurst, J. *Military Collectables*. London, 1983

Martin, P. *Military Costume*. London, 1967

May, W. and Carman, W. Y. *Badges and Insignia of the British Armed Services*. London, 1974

Mollo, A. *Army Uniforms of World War II*. London, 1973

Mollo, J. and McGregor, M. *Uniforms of the American Revolution*. London, 1975

Mollo, L. *Military Fashion*. London, 1972

Nevil, R. *British Military Prints*. London, 1909

Ogilby Trust. *Index to British Military Costume Prints, 1500–1914*. London, 1972

Park, S. and Nafziger, G. *The British Military, 1803–1815*. Cambridge, Ontario, 1983

Parkyn, H. G. *Shoulder belt Plates and Buttons*. London, 1965*

Pika, O. von. *The Armies of Europe Today*. London, 1974

Rankin, R. H. *The Illustrated History of Military Headdress*. London, 1976

Ripley, H. *Buttons of the British Army*. London, 1971*

Rosignoli, G. *Army Badges and Insignia of World War II*. London, 1972

— *Army Badges and Insignia since 1945*. London, 1973

— *The Illustrated Encyclopedia of Military Insignia of the 20th Century*. London, 1987

Simkin, R. and Archer, L. *British Yeomanry Uniforms*. London, 1971

Strachen, H. *British Military Uniforms, 1768–96*. London, 1975

Swinson, A. (ed.). *A Register of the Regiments and Corps of the British Army*. London, 1972

Thorburn, W. T. *Uniforms of the Scottish Infantry, 1740–1900*. Edinburgh, 1970

Walter, J. (ed.). *Arms and Equipment of the British Army, 1866*. London, 1986

Westlake, R. *The Rifle Volunteers*. Chippenham, 1982

— *The Territorial Force, 1914*. Gwent, 1989

White, A. S. *A Bibliography of Regimental Histories of the British Army*. London, 1965

Wilkinson, F. *Badges of the British Army*. London, 1988*

— *Collecting Military Antiques*. London, 1976

— *Militaria*. London, 1969

Wilkinson-Latham, C. *Uniform*

and Weapons in the Zulu War. London, 1977

Wise, T. *A Guide to Military Museums*. Hemel Hempstead, 1971*

Wright, R. J. *Collecting Volunteer Militaria*. Newton Abbot, 1974

The 'Men-at-Arms' Series of booklets, published by Osprey Publishing Company, London, cover an enormous range of military topics – there are more than 250 titles. Each volume is devoted to some aspect of military history, regiments, campaigns or equipment. They comprise a brief history and details of the particular topic, black-and-white photographs and some colour plates. In general their standards are high although, since no researcher is infallible, there are occasional errors.

Magazines

There are many magazines and other publications devoted to various aspects of the topic and most public libraries can supply details of current publications. Some established publications that may be of interest are:

Deutsches Waffen Journal
Diana Armi
Guns and Weapons
Man-at-Arms
Military Hobbies Illustrated
Military Illustrated
Military Modelling
Practical Wargamer
Tac Armi
Tradition (Paris)
Wargame Illustrated
Wargame World

Specialist Publications

Armentaria (Delft, Holland)
Armi Antiche (Turin)
The Artilleryman (Arlington, USA)
The Bulletin of the Military Historical Society
Dispatch (Glasgow)
The Hammer (Burlington, Wisconsin)
Journal of the Royal Artillery
Journal of the Society For Army Historical Research
Militaria Belgica (Brussels)
Revue (Belgium)

Museum publications

Several of the major military museums issue annual publications and among these are: Musée de l'Armée (Paris); Livrustkammaren (Stockholm); Tojhusmuseet (Copenhagen); National Army Museum (London).

Price Guide

The demand for British Army cap badges has grown over the years and shows no sign of abating. Auction prices have risen, and to these prices must be added the dealer's profit margin.

This list was compiled in early 1997 and comes with the usual but vital warning that it is likely to be a little out of date by the time that it is published. This version quotes prices much higher than in previous lists, but that is the trend of the market.

The figure suggested is that which might be paid for a genuine item in very good condition with no damage. Wear and damage must inevitably reduce the price.

Re-strikes should not be offered at anything like these prices.

1	£250	25	£3	49	£2	73	£20
2	£250	26	£2	50	£1	74	£50
3	£450	27	£3	51	£30	75	£15
4	£300	28	£30*	52	£60	76	£40
5	£400	29	£1	53	£15	77	£100
6	£600	30	£5	54	£5	78	£30
7	£600	31	£75	55	£5	79	£40
8	£400	32	£5	56	£10	80	£10
9	£150	33	£5	57	£150	81	£20
10	£400	34	£50	58	£50	82	£10
11	£300	35	£75	59	£5	83	£5
12	£600	36	£60	60	£5	84	£10
13	£250	37	£60	61	£8	85	£3
14	£350	38	£60	62	£50	86	£5
15	£125	39	£1	63	£10	87	£20**
16	£200	40	£5	64	£10	88	£5
17	£60	41	£5	65	£15	89	£15
18	£300	42	£5	66	£15	90	£10
19	£70	43	£75	67	£75	91	£100
20	£80	44	£5	68	£3	92	£20
21	£5	45	£5	69	£5	93	£15
22	£5	46	£5	70	£5	94	£10
23	£5	47	£5	71	£5	95	—
24	£50	48	£1	72	£35	96	£75

* Field Service cap rather than collar   ** H. M. Silver £200

97	£5	144	£15	191	£7	238	£10
98	£35	145	£125	192	£7	239	£10
99	£50	146	£15	193	£20	240	£15
100	£25	147	£10	194	£25	241	£45
101	£15	148	£5	195	£40	242	£25
102	£8	149	£5	196	£5	243	£30
103	£7	150	£15	197	£8	244	£30
104	£10	151	£5	198	£75	245	£12
105	£20	152	£10	199	£10	246	£10
106	£25	153	£10	200	£10	247	£15
107	£15	154	£5	201	£10	248	£50
108	£15	155	£5	202	£25	249	£30
109	£20	156	£5	203	£50	250	£40
110	£60	157	£5	204	£10	251	£20
111	£15	158	£5	205	£100	252	£15
112	£15	159	£40	206	£10*	253	£20
113	£15	160	£35	207	£45	254	£40
114	£15	161	£10	208	£15	255	£20
115	£15	162	£2	209	£8	256	£10
116	£15	163	£5	210	£8	257	£20
117	£35	164	£80	211	£8	258	£25
118	£25	165	£15	212	£45	259	£15
119	£10	166	£25	213	£15	260	£10
120	£10	167	£15	214	£15	261	£5
121	£5	168	£10	215	£20	262	£25
122	£15	169	£15	216	£5	263	£150
123	£10	170	£15	217	£5	264	£50
124	£20	171	£10	218	£25	265	£25
125	£35	172	£75	219	£25	266	£30
126	£35	173	£15	220	£10	267	£45
127	£10	174	£20	221	£10	268	£40
128	£60	175	£15	222	£10	269	£45
129	£40	176	£30	223	£45	270	£10
130	£20	177	£15	224	£35	271	£25
131	£25	178	£15	225	£25	272	£45
132	£10	179	£15	226	£10	273	£1*
133	£20	180	£10	227	£15	274	£30
134	£10	181	£20	228	£25	275	£30
135	£10	182	£7	229	£20	276	£15
136	£5	183	£15	230	£20	277	£35
137	£75	184	£7	231	£10	278	£50
138	£125	185	£20	232	£10	279	£10
139	£15	186	£7	233	£35	280	£10
140	£10	187	£5	234	£35	281	£20
141	£10	188	£7	235	£50	282	£10
142	£75	189	£7	236	£20	283	£10
143	£50	190	£7	237	£10	284	£15

285	£5	323	£7	361	£15	399	£10
286	£5	324	£25	362	£35	400	£10
287	£10	325	£12	363	£25	401	£7
288	£15	326	£12	364	£15	402	£10
289	£10	327	£35	365	£15	403	£10
290	£8	328	£35	366	£15	404	£8
291	£15	329	£15	367	£7	405	£12
292	£7	330	£15	368	£7	406	£15
293	£7	331	£75	369	£10	407	£7
294	£20	332	£45	370	£10	408	£12
295	£8	333	£15	371	£8	409	£12
296	£8	334	£20	372	£8	410	£7
297	£8	335	£7	373	£7	411	£30
298	£7	336	£10	374	£7	412	£7
299	£7	337	£15	375	£15	413	£7
300	£7	338	£15	376	£25	414	£15
301	£8	339	£25	377	£25	415	£8
302	£25	340	£15	378	£7	416	£10
303	£15	341	£25	379	£8	417	£10
304	£8	342	£20	380	£7	418	£7
305	£10	343	£35	381	£7	419	£12
306	£8	344	£7	382	£12	420	£10
307	£20	345	£7	383	£8	421	£8
308	£10	346	£20	384	£10	422	£4
309	£35	347	£15	385	£35	423	£10
310	£40	348	£5	386	£10	424	£15
311	£7	349	£8	387	£10	425	£175
312	£7	350	£7	388	£20	426	£20
313	£20	351	£12	389	£10	427	£12
314	£25	352	£25	390	£7	428	£15
315	£10	353	£45	391	£45	429	£10
316	£30	354	£5	392	£7	430	£25
317	£15	355	£7	393	£12	431	£25
318	£7	356	£35	394	£10	432	£15
319	£7	357	£35	395	£75	433	£60
320	£7	358	£15	396	£45	434	£10
321	£7	359	£8	397	£5	435	£10
322	£10	360	£10	398	£5	436	£15

1. The 17th (Leicestershire) Regiment of Foot. Other ranks' shoulder belt plate, late 18th century. Brass.

2. The 11th (North Devon) Regiment of Foot. Other ranks' shoulder belt plate, 18th century. Brass.

3. The Devizes Association (early 19th-century volunteer unit). Shoulder belt plate, incorporating castle from town's coat of arms. Gilded brass.

4. Officers' helmet plate for the 1812, Waterloo Pattern shako. Gilded. Regiments with special badges had the emblems impressed below a smaller cipher.

5. London and Westminster Light Horse Volunteers. Shoulder belt plate, late 18th century. White metal.

6. The Royal East India Volunteers, 2nd Regiment (London volunteer unit). Shoulder belt plate. Gilded, hallmarked for 1796.

7. The Loyal Chelmsford Volunteers (formed 1803). Shoulder belt plate. Gilded.

8. The 2nd (Queen's Royal) Regiment of Foot. Officers' shoulder belt plate. Silver, hallmarked for 1791.

9

10

12

13

9. The 62nd (The Wiltshire) Regiment of Foot. Other ranks' shoulder belt plate, *circa* 1840. Stamped brass.

10. The 41st (Welch) Regiment of Foot. Officers' shoulder belt plate. The blue enamel centre was introduced in 1831.

11. The 9th (The East Norfolk) Regiment of Foot. Shoulder belt plate. The separate figure of Britannia is pinned to the plate. Brass.

12. The 25th (The King's Own Borderers) Regiment of Foot. Elaborate shoulder belt plate, *circa* 1850. A slider was also worn on the belt.

13. The 9th (The East Norfolk) Regiment of Foot. Other ranks' shoulder belt plate. Pressed brass.

14. The 86th (Royal County Down) Regiment of Foot. Other ranks' shoulder belt plate, *circa* 1850. It was attached to the belt by four broad hooks instead of the more usual two hooks and two lugs. Pressed brass.

11

14

15

16

18

19

15. The Bloomsbury Rifles, raised in 1860; later became a Volunteer Battalion in The Rifle Brigade. Bronze-coloured helmet plate.

16. The Norfolk Regiment. Home Service Pattern helmet plate. Central Britannia and motto in white metal. King's crown dates this to post-1902.

17. The Norfolk Regiment. Other ranks' shako plate with typical double dome of Queen Victoria's crown (QVC); worn 1869–79.

18. The 24th County of London Battalion. Home Service Pattern helmet plate with King's crown; central paschal lamb mounted on red material.

19. The 4th Volunteer Battalion, The Queen's Royal West Surrey Regiment. Belt fitting with QVC and a threaded screw fitting. White metal.

20. The 7th City of London Battalion, The London Regiment. Formed in 1908. Other ranks' Full Dress helmet plate.

17

20

24

31

35

38

21. The Tank Corps. One of a pair of opposite-facing collar badges or 'dogs'.
22. The Northamptonshire Regiment. Collar badge.
23. The Lincolnshire Regiment. Collar badge.
24. The 4th Volunteer Battalion, The Royal West Surrey Regiment. Shooting badge worn on left sleeve of tunic. White metal.
25. The King's Own (Royal Lancaster Regiment). Collar dog.
26. Royal Air Force Volunteer Reserve. Collar dog. Brass.
27. The Gordon Highlanders. Collar dog.
28. The Bloomsbury Rifles. Collar dog, *circa* 1900. White metal.
29. The 7th City of London Battalion. Flaming grenade collar dog.
30. The Norfolk Regiment. Collar dog.
31. The 10th (North Lincoln) Regiment of Foot. Waist belt clasp, pre-1881. Bimetal.
32. Oxford University Officer's Training Corps (Cavalry). Collar dog. White metal.
33. The Hertfordshire and Bedfordshire Yeomanry. Collar dog. Bimetal.
34. The 80th (Staffordshire Volunteers) Regiment of Foot. Numeral worn on the round, 'pork-pie' Undress cap. Brass.
35. The 66th (Berkshire) Regiment of Foot. Waist belt clasp, pre-1881. Bimetal.
36. The Norfolk Regiment. Waist belt clasp, *circa* 1900. Bimetal.
37. The Norfolk Regiment. Waist belt clasp, pre-1881.
38. The Royal Fusiliers. Victorian waist belt clasp.

43

52

56

39. The Duke of Cornwall's Light Infantry. Other ranks' tunic button, post-1929.

40. Royal Engineers' Department. Officers' button with QVC and cipher. Gilded.

41. Although similar to military buttons, this is an early London Post Office button.

42. Ordnance Store. Officers' button, *circa* 1880. Gilded.

43. The Westminster Volunteers. Belt fitting, 19th century. White metal.

44. General Officers' button, 19th century. Gilded.

45. Oxford University Rifle Volunteers (OURV). Button, mid 19th century. White metal.

46. Medical Staff. Officers' button, *circa* 1880. Gilded.

47. Cinque Port Rifle Volunteers. Button, late 19th century. White metal.

48. The Royal Air Force. Other ranks' button, pre-1953. Brass.

49. RAF. Officers' button of same period.

50. The Air Training Corps. Button. White metal.

51. The Holborn Battalion, The Rifle Volunteers. Lapel badge.

52. The 38th Corps of Rifle Volunteers (formed in 1860). Belt fitting. As this badge uses the title 'Artists' it must post-date 1877 when this distinction was introduced.

53. British Airborne Forces. Shoulder patch, Second World War. Cloth.

54. Lapel brooch for those who rendered special services during the First World War; each is numbered on the back. White metal.

55. London Metropolitan Special Constabulary. Cap badge, pre-1953. White metal.

56. The 28th County of London Battalion (Artists Rifles). Second pattern badge.

57

58

61

63

64

66

67

68

69

70

71

57. The 2nd (Queen's Royal) Regiment of Foot. Shako plate. Bimetal.
58. The Second (Queen's Royal) Regiment of Foot. Shako plate, Brass.
59. Regimental numeral. Brass.
60. Shoulder title. Brass.
61. Badge adopted in 1924. Gilding metal.
62. 4th Volunteer Battalion of the regiment. White metal.
63. Forage cap badge, 1898–1921. Bimetal.
64. 22nd County of London Battalion (The Queen's). 1908–22.
65. Cranleigh School Cadet Force. One of the Officer's Training Corps, known from 1948 as the Combined Cadet Force.
66. Badge worn as a unit of the Territorial Force, 1908–21. Blackened brass.
67. The 3rd Volunteer Battalion, The East Surrey Regiment. With QVC. Bronze.
68. The Queen's Regiment. Badge introduced in 1966. Anodized.
69. Collar dog of this regiment, worn 1908–22.
70. Badge of The Queen's Royal Surrey Regiment, formed when The Queen's Royal Regiment (West Surrey) and The East Surrey Regiment were amalgamated in 1959. Anodized.
71. Another version of the collar dog.
72. The 4th Volunteer Battalion, The East Surrey Regiment. Bronze.

73

74

76

78

79

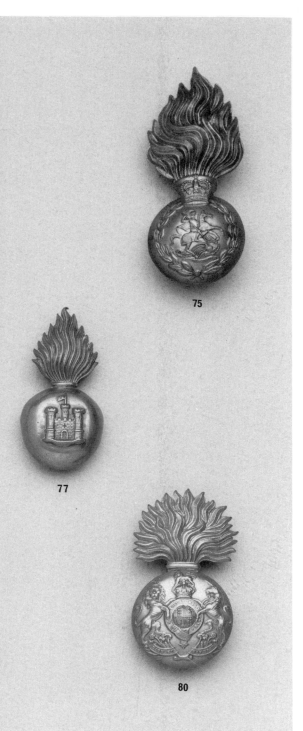

73. The Royal Fusiliers (City of London Regiment). Other ranks' grenade badge for the busby-like racoon skin head-dress worn by the various Fusilier regiments post-1901. Brass.
74. The Royal Irish Fusiliers (Princess Victoria's). Brass.
75. The Northumberland Fusiliers. Brass.
76. The Royal Welsh Fusiliers. Brass.
77. The Royal Inniskilling Fusiliers. Officers' glengarry badge, post-1881. Brass.
78. The Royal Fusiliers (City of London Regiment). Similar to **73**, but with QVC.
79. The Lancashire Fusiliers. White metal.
80. The Royal Scots Fusiliers (with KC).

81 82 83 84

86 87 88

90 91 92

95 96

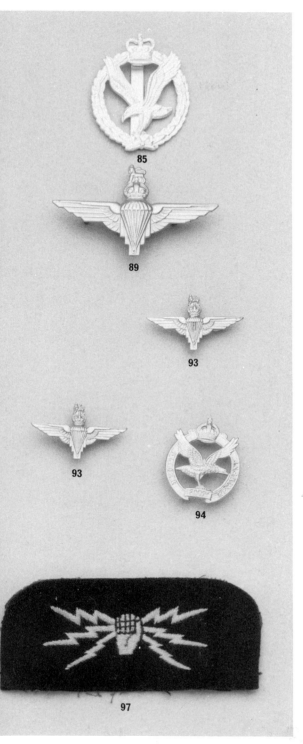

81. The Royal Flying Corps. Unusual other ranks' badge with slider. Brass.

82. RFC. The more usual form, with lugs to secure it to cap.

83. RAF. Cap badge with KC. Brass.

84. RAF. Cap badge introduced in 1942. Plastic, secured by two bendable brass strips.

85. The Army Air Corps, 1957. Anodized.

86. RAF. Cap badge with QC, 1953. Brass.

87. The Army Air Corps, worn 1942–50. Unusual in that it is of hallmarked silver.

88. RAF. Physical Training Instructors' sleeve badge. Brass.

89. The Parachute Regiment. Badge worn from 1943 until 1953 when QC was adopted. White metal.

90. RAF. Officers' badge for peaked cap.

91. RAF. Officers' Dress helmet badge. Bimetal.

92. The Glider Pilot Regiment. Badge with slider adopted in 1955. Anodized.

93. The Parachute Regiment. Collar dogs, pre-1953.

94. The Glider Pilot Regiment. Earlier version.

95. Special Air Service Regiment. Brass badge with wire fittings.

96. SAS. Badge worn from 1953. Bimetal.

97. RAF. Sleeve badge worn by Wireless Operators, Radio and Wireless Mechanics. Cloth.

98

99

100

102

103

104

107

108

109

112

113

114

101

105 **106**

110 **111**

115 **116**

98. Leeds Rifles (Cockburn High School Cadets). Brass.
99. The 5th (Cinque Ports) Battalion, The Royal Sussex Regiment. White metal.
100. The 6th City of London Battalion (City of London Rifles). Bronze.
101. The 5th City of London Battalion (Rifle Brigade). White metal.
102. The Rifle Brigade (Prince Consort's Own). Badge worn 1934–57. White metal.
103. The King's Royal Rifle Corps. With KC. Black.
104. The Buckinghamshire Battalion, The Oxfordshire and Buckinghamshire Light Infantry. Black.
105. 3/4th County of London Yeomanry (Sharpshooters). Bimetal.
106. The 23rd County of London Battalion, The London Regiment. Bimetal.
107. The 16th County of London Battalion (Queen's Westminster Rifles). Worn 1908–22. Black.
108. The Queen's Royal Rifles. Worn 1961. Brass.
109. The 9th County of London Battalion (Queen Victoria's). Brass.
110. The 3rd County of London (Sharp Shooters) Imperial Yeomanry.
111. The 7th City of London Battalion. Bimetal.
112. The 11th County of London Battalion (Finsbury Rifles). Brass.
113. The 12th County of London Battalion (The Rangers). Black.
114. The King's Royal Rifle Corps Cadets. The motto *Celer et Audax* beneath the crown replaced by *Fight the Good Fight* and *CLB Cadets.*
115. The 21st County of London Battalion (First Surrey Rifles). Black.
116. The 3rd County of London Yeomanry (The Sharpshooters) (Hussars).

117

118

120

121

123

125

126

117. The Cameronians (Scottish Rifles). Piper's badge, 1921–68. White metal.
118. The Northumberland Fusiliers: 20th, 21st, 22nd and 29th Battalions (Tyneside Scottish), 1914–18. White metal.
119. The Scottish Horse. A composite badge, possibly for a slouch hat.
120. The Cameronians (Scottish Rifles). White metal.
121. The Lowland Brigade. Worn 1959–68. Anodized.
122. Lovat's Scouts. Worn 1903–20. White metal.
123. The 9th (Glasgow Highlanders) Battalion, The Highland Light Infantry (City of Glasgow Regiment). Post-1953. White metal.
124. The 10th (Scottish) Battalion, The King's (Liverpool) Regiment. Worn 1908–37. White metal.
125. The Highland Regiment. Other ranks' badge worn from 1942 until disbanded in 1949. White metal.
126. The Lowland Regiment. Similar dates. White metal.
127. The Seaforth Highlanders (Ross-shire Buffs, The Duke of Albany's). Badge worn 1898–1921. White metal.

128

129

133

134

135

137

138

128. The Militia Artillery. Helmet plate worn from 1891 when the title Militia Artillery replaced Artillery Militia. White metal.

129. The Territorial Force. Artillery helmet plate. Laurel spray above gun replaces motto *Ubique* found on plates of the regular units.

130. The Honourable Artillery Company. Officers' forage cap badge, post-1902. Gilded.

131. The Honourable Artillery Company. Worn by Warrant Officers and sergeants. Initials in white metal.

132. The Honourable Artillery Company. Other ranks' cap badge. Brass.

133. The Royal Horse Artillery. Collar dog with KC, 1936–53.

134/5. The Royal Horse Artillery. A pair of collar dogs with QC, 1953.

136. Royal Artillery. Cap badge with KC. Brass.

137. A Cadet Company. Helmet plate with QVC so pre-1901.

138. Cinque Ports Artillery Volunteers. Helmet plate with QVC.

139. Royal Malta Artillery. With KC.

140. Royal Artillery. Badge with KC. Wheel on gun mounted separately.

141

143

145

142

144

146

141. The Royal Marine Light Infantry. Helmet plate worn from 1905. Brass.

142. The Royal East Middlesex Militia. Glengarry badge, 1874–81. White metal.

143. The Royal Malta Militia. Shako plate with KC. Bimetal.

144. The 11th (Royal Militia Island of Jersey) Battalion, The Hampshire Regiment. This unit was only in being from 1940 until 1946.

145. The Middlesex Regiment. Helmet plate with KC (lacking top cross). Bimetal.

146. The Royal Malta Militia. Bimetal.

147

148

149

151

152

153

155

156

157

159

160

161

150

154

158

162   **163**

147. The Royal Engineers. Forage cap badge with cipher of King George V. The centre was left unvoided as an economy measure during the First World War.

148. Similar badge, with cipher of King George VI and voided centre.

149. Similar badge with cipher of white metal.

150. The Machine Gun Corps. Cap badge, 1915–22.

151. The Royal Army Medical Corps. Cap badge with KC. Brass.

152. RAMC. Badge with St Edward's crown, adopted 1953. Bimetal.

153. The Army Service Corps. Badge worn from 1916 until 1918 when the prefix Royal was added. Brass.

154. The Machine Gun Corps. Officers' collar dog. Bronze.

155. RAMC. Badge with St. Edward's crown, adopted in 1953. Brass.

156. Royal Army Service Corps. Badge with King George VI cipher and voided centre.

157. The Royal Corps of Transport, formed in 1965. Anodized.

158. Crossed axes worn by pioneers in the Infantry, and in some units combined with grenade (Guards), a star (Scots and Irish Guards) and a bugle (light infantry or rifle regiments). Brass.

159. The School of Musketry. Badge worn 1902–19.

160. The Army Physical Training Staff. Forage cap badge worn from 1902.

161. Smaller version of same badge.

162. What appears to be a British collar dog is in fact Belgian. Take care!

163. Artificers' badge worn by armourer sergeants, machinery artificers and smiths.

164

165

166

168

169

170

172

173

174

176

177

178

167

171

175

179

164. The 1/1st London Divisional Cyclist Company, formed in 1916. Voided badge. Brass.

165. The Army Cyclist Corps, formed in 1914. The wheel has 16 spokes; another version has 12. Brass.

166. The 25th County of London (Cyclist) Battalion. Brass.

167. The 15th County of London Battalion (Prince of Wales's Own Civil Service Rifles). Badge worn from 1908. Brass.

168. Inns of Court OTC, incorporating the badges of the various Inns or legal centres of London. Brass.

169. The 5th City of London Battalion (London Rifle Brigade), Cadets. Post-1908. Brass.

170. The Westminster (Yeomanry) Dragoons. Badge worn 1908–22. White metal.

171. The 13th County of London Battalion (Kensington).

172. The Paddington Rifles, 1908–12 when it was replaced by The 10th County of London Regiment (Hackney).

173. The 19th County of London Battalion (St Pancras). Brass.

174. The 20th County of London Battalion (Blackheath and Woolwich). Bimetal.

175. The 18th County of London Battalion (London Irish Rifles). White metal.

176. City of London Imperial Yeomanry (Rough Riders). Bimetal.

177. The 14th County of London Battalion (London Scottish). Worn 1908. White metal.

178. The 10th County of London Battalion (Hackney), post-1912. This unit replaced The Paddington Rifles (see 172). Brass.

179. The 28th County of London Battalion (Artists' Rifles). White metal.

180

181

184

185

186

187

190

191

192

194

195

196

197

198

182

183

188

189

193

199

180. The Life Guards. Centre voided with cipher of King George VI. This unit was formed in 1922 when the 1st and 2nd Life Guards were amalgamated.

181. The 2nd Life Guards, with cipher of King George V, first issued in 1914. Brass.

182. The Scots Guards. Brass.

183. The Scots Guards. Badge worn by sergeants and musicians. White metal.

184. The Life Guards, with cipher of Queen Elizabeth II, post-1953.

185. The 1st Life Guards.

186. The Royal Horse Guards (The Blues), post-1953.

187. The Blues and Royals. Regiment formed in 1969 by amalgamation of The Royal Horse Guards (The Blues) and The Royal Dragoons (1st Dragoons). Brass.

188. Irish Guards. Brass.

189. The Coldstream Guards. Other ranks', 1905–. Brass.

190. The Household Cavalry. Cipher of Queen Elizabeth II.

191. The Grenadier Guards. Flaming grenade; plain for other ranks.

192. The Grenadier Guards. Similar, but with lugs in place of the slider.

193. The Scots Guards. Badge with lugs for attachment to belt or pouch. White metal.

194. The Grenadier Guards. With impressed GR cipher mirrored. Worn by sergeants.

195. The Grenadier Guards. Royal cipher applied and not impressed. Worn by sergeants and commissioned quartermasters. White metal.

196. The Welsh Guards. Shoulder title. White metal.

197. The Welsh Guards. Cap badge worn from 1915 when the regiment was formed. Brass.

198. The Welsh Guards. Badge worn on the puggaree. Brass.

199. The Grenadier Guards. This badge was also worn on the puggaree or, as shown, with the initials GG as a shoulder title. Brass.

200

201

203

204

206

207

208

209

210

211

213

214

216

217

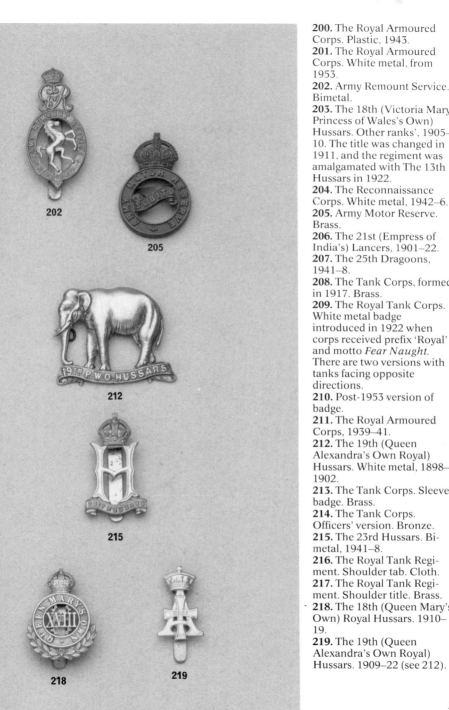

200. The Royal Armoured Corps. Plastic, 1943.

201. The Royal Armoured Corps. White metal, from 1953.

202. Army Remount Service. Bimetal.

203. The 18th (Victoria Mary, Princess of Wales's Own) Hussars. Other ranks', 1905–10. The title was changed in 1911, and the regiment was amalgamated with The 13th Hussars in 1922.

204. The Reconnaissance Corps. White metal, 1942–6.

205. Army Motor Reserve. Brass.

206. The 21st (Empress of India's) Lancers, 1901–22.

207. The 25th Dragoons, 1941–8.

208. The Tank Corps, formed in 1917. Brass.

209. The Royal Tank Corps. White metal badge introduced in 1922 when corps received prefix 'Royal' and motto *Fear Naught*. There are two versions with tanks facing opposite directions.

210. Post-1953 version of badge.

211. The Royal Armoured Corps, 1939–41.

212. The 19th (Queen Alexandra's Own Royal) Hussars. White metal, 1898–1902.

213. The Tank Corps. Sleeve badge. Brass.

214. The Tank Corps. Officers' version. Bronze.

215. The 23rd Hussars. Bimetal, 1941–8.

216. The Royal Tank Regiment. Shoulder tab. Cloth.

217. The Royal Tank Regiment. Shoulder title. Brass.

218. The 18th (Queen Mary's Own) Royal Hussars. 1910–19.

219. The 19th (Queen Alexandra's Own Royal) Hussars. 1909–22 (see 212).

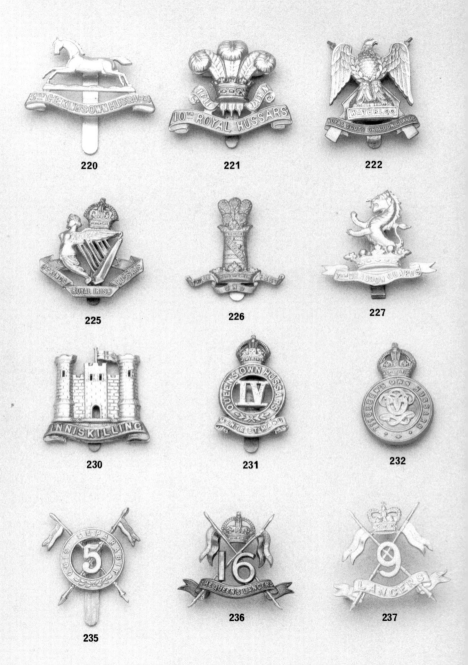

220

221

222

225

226

227

230

231

232

235

236

237

220. The 3rd (King's Own) Hussars. Bimetal, 1920–58.
221. The 10th Royal Hussars. Bimetal, 1896–1969.
222. The Royal Scots Dragoon Guards. Bimetal, 1971.
223. The 14th (King's) Hussars. Until 1915.
224. The 6th Dragoon Guards (Carabineers). Bimetal, 1902–22.
225. The 8th (King's Royal Irish) Hussars. Bimetal, 1904–54.
226. The 11th (Prince Albert's Own) Hussars. Until 1969.
227. The 7th (The Princess Royal's) Dragoon Guards. 1898–1906.
228. The 15th (The King's) Hussars. Bimetal, 1902–22.
229. The 1st (Royal) Dragoons. 1902–22.
230. The 6th (Inniskilling) Dragoons. Bimetal, until 1922.
231. The 4th (Queen's Own) Hussars. 1907–54.
232. The 7th (Queen's Own) Hussars. 1901–55.
233. The 5th (Princess Charlotte of Wales's) Dragoon Guards. Bimetal, 1902–22.
234. The 13th Hussars. Bimetal, 1902–22.
235. The 5th (Royal Irish) Lancers. Bimetal, 1896–22.
236. The 16th (The Queen's) Lancers. Bimetal, 1905–22.
237. The 9th Queen's Royal Lancers. Anodized, 1954–60.
238. The 12th Royal Lancers (Prince of Wales's). Bimetal, 1930–54.
239. The Royal Dragoons (1st Dragoons). Bimetal, 1949–69.

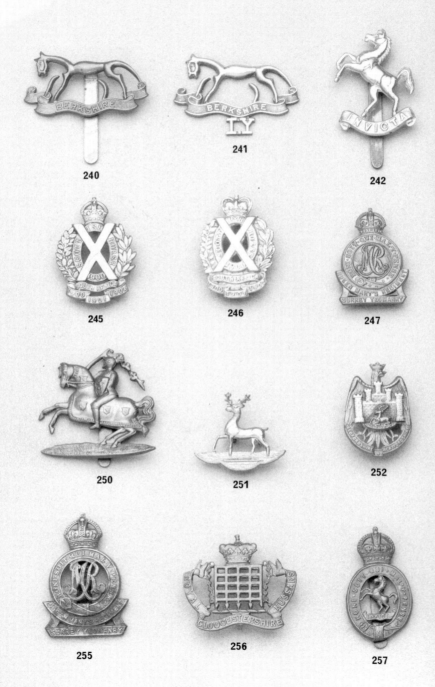

240

241

242

245

246

247

250

251

252

255

256

257

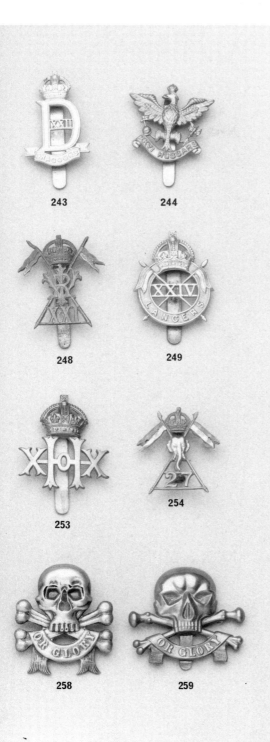

240. The Royal Berkshire (Hungerford) Yeomanry (Dragoons). Brass, 1908–22.
241. Berkshire Imperial Yeomanry. White metal, 1901–08.
242. The Queen's Own West Kent Yeomanry (Hussars). 1908–22.
243. The 22nd Dragoons. White metal, 1940–8.
244. The 26th Hussars. Brass, 1940–8.
245. The Scottish Horse. Raised in 1900 for the Imperial Yeomanry. Brass.
246. Similar badge with Scottish crown. White metal.
247. The Queen Mary's Surrey Yeomanry (Lancers). 1910–22. White metal.
248. The 21st (Empress of India's) Lancers. Economy brass issue from 1916.
249. The 24th Lancers. White metal, 1940–8.
250. The Fife and Forfarshire Yeomanry (Dragoons). Found in brass and white metal, 1908–22.
251. The Hertfordshire Yeomanry (Dragoons). Brass, 1908–22.
252. The Bedfordshire and Hertfordshire Regiment. Bimetal, 1919–58.
253. The 20th Hussars. 1908–22. Brass.
254. The 27th Lancers. Bimetal, 1940–8.
255. The Queen Mary's Surrey Yeomanry (Lancers). With voided centre (see 247).
256. The Royal Gloucestershire Hussars (a unit of the Imperial Yeomanry). 1902–8.
257. The Duke of Connaught's Own Royal East Kent Yeomanry (Mounted Rifles). 1908–22.
258. The 17th (Duke of Cambridge's Own) Lancers. NCOs' arm badge. White metal.
259. Similar badge in brass. In 1922 the regiment was amalgamated with The 21st (Empress of India's) Lancers to form The 17th/21st Lancers.

260

261

262

264

265

267

266

269

270

271

273

274

275

276

263

268

272

277

260. The Royal Irish Rifles. White metal, 1913–52. The title was changed to The Royal Ulster Rifles in 1920.
261. The Royal Irish Rangers. Anodized, 1968.
262. The North Irish Horse. Brass, 1908–52.
263. The Dublin County Light Infantry. Glengarry badge, post-1881. White metal.
264. The Connaught Rangers. Officers' badge, 1902–22. Bronze.
265. The 8th Irish Battalion, The King's (Liverpool Regiment). Brass, 1908–21.
266. The Connaught Rangers. Brass, 1902–22.
267. The Northumberland Fusiliers: 24th–27th and 30th Battalions (Tyneside Irish), 1914–18. Brass.
268. The Dublin Regiment National Volunteers. Brass.
269. The Royal Dublin Fusiliers. Officers' badge, 1881–1922. Bronze.
270. The North of Ireland Imperial Yeomanry. Collar dog, 1901–8. White metal.
271. The Royal Dublin Fusiliers. Bimetal, 1881–1922.
272. The 14th Battalion (Young Citizens), The Royal Irish Rifles. Brass, 1914–18.
273. The Royal Ulster Rifles. White metal, 1920. Doubtful if original badge.
274. The Royal Munster Fusiliers. Bimetal, 1898–1921.
275. The Prince of Wales's Leinster Regiment (Royal Canadians). Bimetal, 1881–1922.
276. The Royal Inniskilling Fusiliers. Bimetal, 1881–1958; except during the late 1920s and early 1930s when the grenade was discarded.
277. The South Irish Horse. Brass, 1908–22.

278   279

282   283

285   286

288   289

278. The King's Own Scottish Borderers. White metal, 1887–1902.

279. The King's Own Scottish Borderers. White metal, post–1902.

280. The Highland Light Infantry. With small scroll, white metal, 1902–52.

281. The Highland Light Infantry. With large scroll, white metal, 1902–52.

282. The Queen's Own Cameron Highlanders. White metal, 1898–1961.

283. The Queen's Own Cameron Highlanders. Badge for feather bonnet and glengarry. White metal.

284. The Queen's Own Cameron Highlanders (The Liverpool Scottish). White metal, post-1938.

285. The Argyll and Sutherland Highlanders (Princess Louise's). Officers' collar dog. Bronze.

286. The Argyll and Sutherland Highlanders (Princess Louise's). Other ranks' collar dog. White metal.

287. The Royal Scots (Royal Regiment). Bimetal with red (1st Battalion) or green (2nd Battalion) cloth backing at centre, 1920–58, and from 1969.

288. The Princess Louise's (Argyll and Sutherland Highlanders). White metal with solid centre, 1882–1900.

289. Similar, but with voided centre.

290. The Highland Brigade. Anodized, 1959–68.

291. Oxford University OTC (Infantry). White metal.
292. The King's (Shropshire Light Infantry). Bimetal.
293. The Duke of Cornwall's Light Infantry. White metal.
294. The Women's Army Auxiliary Corps, formed in 1917. Brass.
295. Auxiliary Territorial Service (women's service formed in 1938). Brass.
296. Prince Albert's (Somerset Light Infantry). White metal.
297. Prince Albert's (Somerset Light Infantry): 4th and 5th Battalions.
298. The Durham Light Infantry. White metal, 1902–53.
299. The Royal Observer Corps.
300. The York and Lancaster Regiment. Bimetal, 1881–1969.
301. The Cambridgeshire Regiment. Formed in 1908. Bimetal. The title is also found spelt as Cambridgshire.
302. The Women's Legion. Formed in 1915 and absorbed into the WAAC in 1917. White metal.
303. The Women's Land Army. Reformed in 1939. With green enamel centre.
304. The King's Own Yorkshire Light Infantry. Bimetal, 1898–1958.
305. The Loyal North Lancashire Regiment. Bimetal, 1901–20.
306. The Loyal (North Lancashire) Regiment. Bimetal, 1921–53.
307. Queen Alexandra's Royal Army Nursing Corps. 1949–53.
308. Queen Mary's Army Auxiliary Corps and Army Territorial Service, Old Comrades' Association.

309

310

311

313

314

315

317

318

319

321

322

323

312

316

320

324

309. The Sherwood Foresters (The Derbyshire Regiment). Bimetal, 1898–1901.
310. The Sherwood Foresters (The Derbyshire Regiment). Belt or pouch fitting. Bimetal.
311. The 4th Battalion, Duke of Edinburgh's (The Wiltshire Regiment). Black, 1916–47.
312. The Border Regiment. White metal, 1901–53.
313. The Sherwood Foresters (Nottinghamshire and Derbyshire Regiment). Officers' badge, 1902–53. Bronze.
314. The Essex Volunteer Regiment. Brass, 1914–18.
315. The East Anglian Brigade. Formed in 1957/8 and changed to The Royal Anglian Regiment in 1968. White metal.
316. The 5th Battalion, The Border Regiment. White metal, with South Africa battle honour.
317. The Northamptonshire Regiment. With castle and flag. Brass, 1898–1921.
318. The Northamptonshire Regiment. Without flag and key. Bimetal.
319. The Essex Regiment. Bronze, 1908–58.
320. The Prince of Wales's Volunteers (The South Lancashire Regiment). Bimetal, 1920–58.
321. The Duke of Cambridge's Own (Middlesex Regiment). Bimetal, 1898–1921.
322. The same badge, but plastic, *circa* 1943.
323. The East Yorkshire Regiment. Bimetal, 1898–1958.
324. The 2nd King Edward's Horse. Brass, 1914–24.

325

326

327

330

331

332

335

336

337

339

340

341

328

329

333

334

338

342

325. The Duke of Lancaster's Own Yeomanry (Dragoons). Brass, 1908–51.

326. The South Nottinghamshire (Yeomanry) Hussars. Brass, 1908–52.

327. Westmoreland and Cumberland Yeomanry. Brass, 1908–22.

328. The Lincolnshire Yeomanry (Lancers). Brass, 1908–22.

329. The Prince Albert's Own Leicestershire Yeomanry (Hussars). Brass, 1922–56.

330. The Essex Yeomanry. Brass, 1916–54.

331. The Imperial Yeomanry. General Service badge worn on the slouch hat, 1901–8. Brass, with red and blue rosette.

332. The Duke of Lancaster's Own Yeomanry (Dragoons). Bimetal.

333. The Shropshire Yeomanry. Brass, 1908–50.

334. The Earl of Chester's Cheshire Yeomanry (Hussars). Brass, 1908–22.

335. The Queen's Own (Royal West Kent) Regiment. White metal, 1898–1958.

336. The Queen's Own Yorkshire Yeomanry (Dragoons). White metal, 1951–6.

337. The 1st Battalion, The Monmouthshire Regiment. White metal, 1908–25.

338. The Queen's Own Worcestershire (Yeomanry) Hussars. Bimetal, 1908–56.

339. The Brecknockshire Battalion, The South Wales Borderers. Brass, 1908–22.

340. The Duke of York's Own Loyal Suffolk (Yeomanry) Hussars. Bimetal, 1908–61.

341. The Glamorganshire Yeomanry (Dragoons). Bimetal, 1908–22.

342. The Derbyshire Yeomanry (Dragoons). Brass, 1908–57.

343

344

345

348

349

350

353

354

355

358

359

360

346

347

351

352

356

357

361

362

343. The Dorsetshire Regiment. Bimetal, 1898–1901.
344. The Dorsetshire Regiment. Bimetal, 1901–56.
345. The Royal Warwickshire Regiment. Bimetal, 1898–1958.
346. The Hampshire Yeomanry (Carabineers). Brass, 1916–51.
347. The Northumberland (Yeomanry) Hussars. Brass, 1908–56.
348. The Duke of Wellington's (West Riding Regiment). Officers' collar dog. Bronze.
349. The Prince of Wales's Own (West Yorkshire Regiment). Bimetal, 1898–1958.
350. The Duke of Wellington's (West Riding Regiment). Bimetal, 1897–1970.
351. The Alexandra, Princess of Wales's Own Yorkshire Yeomanry (Hussars). Bimetal, 1908–56.
352. The 2nd Northamptonshire Yeomanry. White metal, 1939–45.
353. Alexandra, Princess of Wales's Own (Yorkshire Regiment). Brass, 1898–1908.
354. The East Lancashire Regiment. Officers' collar dog. Bronze.
355. The East Lancashire Regiment. Bimetal, 1930–54.
356. The Welsh (Yeomanry) Horse (Lancers). Brass, 1914–21.
357. The Pembrokeshire (Castlemain) Yeomanry (Hussars). Bimetal, 1908–71.
358. The Green Howards (Alexandra, Princess of Wales's Own Yorkshire Regiment). Bronze, 1903–50.
359. The King's Regiment (Liverpool). Bimetal, 1927–50.
360. The Green Howards (Alexandra, Princess of Wales's Own Yorkshire Regiment). Badge worn 1950–8, and 1969–. Anodized.
361. The Royal Buckinghamshire (Yeomanry) Hussars. Brass, 1908–52.
362. The Huntingdonshire Cyclist Battalion. Brass, 1914–18. Also The Huntingdonshire Home Guard, 1951–7.

363. The 7th Battalion, The Hampshire Regiment. Brass, 1908–21.

364. The Cheshire Regiment. Bronze, 1898–1921.

365. The Hampshire Regiment. Officers' pattern. Bimetal.

366. The Lancashire Fusiliers. Officers' badge, 1898–1921. Bronze.

367. The Lancashire Fusiliers. Bimetal, 1898–1921.

368. The Hampshire Regiment. Bimetal, 1898–1921.

369. The Royal Hampshire Regiment. Bimetal, 1947–53.

370. The South Wales Borderers. Bimetal, 1898–1969.

371. The Cheshire Regiment. Bimetal, 1898–1921.

372. The Gloucestershire Regiment. Brass badge worn on rear of head-dress.

373. The Gloucestershire Regiment. White metal, 1898–1958.

374. The Lincolnshire Regiment. Bimetal, 1898–1947.

375. The Bedfordshire Regiment. Brass, 1898–1919.

376. The 4th Battalion, The Gloucestershire Regiment. Blackened brass, 1898–1958.

377. The 8th (Isle of Wight Rifles, Princess Beatrice's) Battalion, The Hampshire Regiment. Black, 1908–21.

378. The Suffolk Regiment. Bimetal, 1901–55.

379. The Welsh Regiment. Bimetal, 1898 until 1920 when it became Welch.

380. The Cheshire Regiment. Bimetal, 1898–1921. See 370 with larger scroll.

381. The Cheshire Regiment. Bimetal, 1922–58 and post-1969.

382. The Prince of Wales's (North Staffordshire Regiment). Bronze, 1898–1959.

383. The Leicestershire Regiment. Bimetal, 1898–1951.

384

385

386

388

389

390

392

393

394

395

397

398

387

391

396

399

384. The Army Educational Corps. Brass, 1927–46.
385. Yeomanry Cadets. KC. Brass.
386. Army Apprentices' School. Piper's badge. White metal, 1954.
387. The Royal Naval Mine Watching Service.
388. The Royal Military Academy, Woolwich. Gilded, gilt and bronze, 1902–47.
389. The Royal Military College, Sandhurst. White metal, 1947–53.
390. The Royal Army Pay Corps. Bimetal, 1929–53.
391. Drake Battalion, The Royal Naval Division. Bimetal, 1916–18.
392. The Royal Army Educational Corps. Bimetal, 1946–54.
393. The Royal Army Educational Corps. Bimetal, 1954–.
394. The Mobile Defence Corps. Bimetal, 1955–9.
395. The Royal Army Pay Corps. Brass, 1920–29.
396. Anson Battalion, The Royal Naval Division. Brass, 1916–18.
397. The Army Catering Corps. Bimetal, 1941–54.
398. The Army Catering Corps. Brass, 1941–54.
399. Royal Navy. Officers' cap badge.

400

401

402

404

405

406

409

410

411

414

415

416

403

408

407

413

412

417

400. The Manchester Regiment. Bimetal, 1898–1923.
401. The Manchester Regiment. Brass, 1923–58. Also in white metal.
402. The Manchester Regiment. Bimetal, 1898–1923. With different style of lettering.
403. The East Anglian Brigade. Anodized, 1958.
404. The Royal Norfolk Regiment. Brass, 1937–58.
405. The Norfolk Regiment. Bimetal, 1898–1937.
406. The Norfolk Regiment. Bronze.
407. The Devonshire Regiment. Bimetal, 1903–55.
408. The Devonshire Regiment. Blackened brass, 1920–47.
409. The Herefordshire Regiment. Bimetal, 1908–47.
410. The Buffs (East Kent Regiment). Brass, 1896–1961.
411. The Herefordshire Regiment. Officers' badge. Bronze.
412. The Royal Northumberland Fusiliers. Bimetal, 1935–59.
413. The Worcestershire Regiment. Bimetal, 1925–66.
414. The Suffolk Regiment. Brass, 1901–52.
415. The Worcestershire Regiment. Brass, 1898–1925.
416. The Suffolk Regiment. White metal.
417. The Northumberland Fusiliers. Brass, pre-1935.

418

419

420

423

424

425

428

429

430

432

433

434

418. The Royal Corps of Signals. Bimetal, 1920–47.
419. The Royal Corps of Signals. Officers' badge. Bronze.
420. Army Ordnance Corps. Brass, 1896–1918.
421. The Intelligence Corps. Brass, 1940–55.
422. The Intelligence Corps. Anodized, 1955.
423. The Royal Army Ordnance Corps. Brass, 1918–47.
424. The Royal Army Ordnance Corps. 1947–49.
425. Oxford University OTC (Signals).
426. Army Veterinary Corps. Brass, 1916.
427. Army Veterinary Corps. Bimetal, 1903–18.
428. The Corps of Royal Military Police. Brass, 1948–53.
429. The Corps of Royal Military Police. Bimetal, 1953.
430. The Military Provost Staff Corps. Brass, 1936–53.
431. Navy, Army and Air Force Institutes (NAAFI). Silver plated.
432. Royal Army Chaplains' Department. Collar dog, 1939–53. Bronze.
433. Army Scripture Readers. Bimetal.
434. Royal Army Dental Corps. Bimetal, 1948–54.
435. Royal Army Dental Corps. Brass, 1921–48.
436. Royal Army Dental Corps. Officers' badge. Bronze.

Index to the Plates

Some unit titles have been slightly modified in order to simplify the listing and location of entries, but the relevant captions give the full titles. References are to plate numbers.